Master Your Negotiating Skills

How to Always Come Out On Top

Jared Anderson

Introduction

Often when we think of negotiating and influencing, what comes to mind is the slick car salesman who is churning out every trick in the book to sell you a mediocre yet overpriced car.

As much as we realize that we may be being taken for a ride, the passionate spins of the salesman can be very persuasive. But is there more to negotiating and influencing than just charisma and rhetoric?

The answer is a resounding YES! Understanding basic human psychology is essential to this and in this book we are going to look at some key distinctions and advantages of negotiating skills.

Table of Contents

1. Basic Negotiation Skills You Need to Know
2. The Benefits of Having Good Negotiation Skills
3. Negotiation Skills - Winning As a Seller
4. Negotiating Skills Enhancement
5. 10 Reasons to Improve Your Negotiation Skills
6. Negotiation Skills Training
7. Negotiating Skills and Career Development
8. The Importance of Good Negotiation Skills to Your Business Success
9. Leadership Development Through Negotiation Skills
10. Effective Negotiation Skills

Chapter I

Basic Negotiation Skills You Need to Know

Learning some basic negotiation skills can go a long way in your attempt to be successful in the business market. A good negotiator will be able to save money for their business and potentially make a lot more money in the long run. Here are some of the basic negotiation skills that you need to know.

One of the basic negotiation skills to learn is how to ask for something that you want. Many people go into negotiations and they never actually get around to telling the other person what they want out of the process.

You need to be able to articulate your requirements to the other party so that they can work on fulfilling them. If you do not actually alert them as to what you want, you will most definitely not get it. Even though it might feel awkward, you need to build up the courage to ask them.

Another basic negotiation skill that you need to learn is how to avoid negotiating against yourself. Many people make the mistake of taking the side of the other individual during negotiations.

For example, they will make an offer to the other person and the counter party sits in silence contemplating it for a few seconds. During the silence, the person that made the offer starts to feel awkward and immediately makes another offer.

Instead of negotiating against yourself because you feel awkward during the silence, you need to learn how to sit quietly. After you make an offer, sit there until the other person says something.

When you go into a negotiation, you also need to know what your bottom line is. You need to have a number that is held in the back of your mind that represents the highest amount of money that you would pay for something.

By doing this, you will give yourself a little bit of room to work with and a safety net. You should always start out with a price that is significantly different than your bottom line. Then you can work your way back to that if the other party still wants to negotiate the price.

One of the most important basic negotiation skills that you can develop is the art of listening. You need to sit quietly and attentively when the other person is talking. Pay attention to what they are actually saying and try to determine exactly what they want.

If you can determine exactly what it is that they want, you will have much better chance of giving it to them. If you can give the other person what they want while still getting what you want, the negotiation process will be a success.

Chapter II

The Benefits of Having Good Negotiation Skills

If you're interested in the benefits of possessing good negotiation skills chances are you are a business person, seeking to improve your skills, a timid person, fed up with being at the bottom of the food chain, or the type of person who just likes learning new things.

Few people actually realize negotiating is nearly an every day part of life, the only thing which defines negotiation from "cutting a deal" is the perceived importance to the affected parties.

What exactly are good negotiation skills? We'll explore this question in a manner a little more serious than negotiating "You can go out Friday night if you mow the yard".

A good negotiator must be intelligent, which doesn't mean you're of Einstein IQ, sometimes just the opposite is true. A person must be intelligent enough to realize they are either ignorant or their knowledge is dwarfed by their opponent.

One must be willing to research and perform his due diligence in order to understand the subject and be able to intelligently understand and converse about opponent's proposals.

In order to become a good negotiator one must not only understand human emotions and behavior, but be able to perceive what emotion the opponent is experiencing when they're experiencing it and why. In theory, negotiations should always be void of emotions. The "can't take it personal" attitude, should always rule. Humans have emotions, which some can control or hide better than othe. By analyzing your opponent, a sharp negoiator will have a plan in place to extract reactions to certain questions or situations. You will be able to put yourself in your opponent's place that could grant you insight to his motives and how to address them.

A great negotiator will maintain a reputation of being honest and fair. It doesn't mean he's weak. Many inexperienced or arrogant people placed in the position of negotiating will maintain a staunch position of wanting everything their way, which only creates an adversarial and confrontational atmosphere.

Simple issues will become mammoth obstacles and it quickly becomes a "I'll take my ball and go home" situation where everyone digs their heels in and refuses to bend.

The great negotiator will understand to arrive at a position both parties can live with. He must ultimately present a win - win situation and he'll do everything in his power to prevent a confrontational atmosphere from being created.

I was once involved in a set of contract talks where the situation had become stalemated. The ground rules for any request for a recess had to be made on an alternating basis. In other words, if the company was granted a recess they could not request another one until the union had used one.

I was taken off guard when the union chief negotiator suddenly requested an unexpected recess, then we just sat at the table doing nothing. When the company human resource manager returned to the table the union spokesman asked if he was alright. The man looked surprised and nodded his head yes. The union spokesman replied "Good, I could tell you weren't feeling well so I called a recess."

"I ate something bad at lunch," the man replied. From that point on, because one negotiator displayed a human concern for the others well being over the importance of the contract talks, the logger head was broken and negotiations were quickly resolved.

Chapter III

Negotiation Skills - Winning As a Seller

Just as a buyer can employ certain tactics to strengthen her negotiation position and results, a seller can do certain things to benefit his position and results. It is learned negotiation skills that give a seller advantage and the consistent application of them will pay off over time.

I noted how the buyer in a negotiation usually has the upper hand, because there are more things a buyer can do to successfully to conclude a deal. The reason for this is fairly obvious: a seller has a product or service they need to sell to make money, and in almost every market on the planet, there is substantial competition for that product or service.

Buyers can always go elsewhere and try to get a better deal if they don't like the one they are engaged in. It's what makes selling anything a tough, tough job.

But, there are things a seller can do to help his position. Here we will discuss a few.

1. Make it clear you have the buyer's best interest at heart

This means be sincere and prove it. Using over-baked, cliche ridden lines about how much you care for the buyer will suffer a loss just to make her a great deal - does not cut it. Buyers see through this and it has the reverse affect of what most cheesy sellers are hoping for when they use this method. Buyers want to know the seller is there for something more than simply making money. Buyer's understand why the seller is selling (to make money), so good sellers reveal to buyers there is more to it than just that. Communicating to the buyer that you love what you do, and giving them specific reasons why, will go a long way toward lessening the buyer's concern that he will only be sold the most expensive product at the highest margin.

Make it personal. Tell the buyer you sincerely hope he will be coming back to see you on his next purchase because you hope to establish a strong, ongoing relationship. Few people are so hard nosed they will not react positively to a sincere offer of friendship. As a seller, you can make use of the natural human tendency to want more friendships. And if a buyer sees you as a friend instead of a huckster, he will benefit you with a sale and more to come.

2. Take a "Low Key" approach

A low key approach is self-explanatory. It means "not high key". A high key approach is talking a mile a minute, asking insincere questions, laughing inappropriately and too often, showing the buyer twice as much product as he needs to see and telling him twice as much information as he needs to know until he buys something... just to get rid of you. Interestingly, most people who go into sales naturally take this approach with buyers. And it usually does not work.

A low key approach is vital for a seller seeking to use negotiation skills to ensure a profitable outcome. This seller reminds the buyer he is there to assist him - not push her. He suggests products or services that may meet his needs and if they don't, he will gladly refer him elsewhere. He reminds him he wants him to be happy, but not so that he makes a fat commission or profit, but so that he considers him a consultant, someone to whom he will come back to for counsel, or advice.

3. Apply the lever of time

A buyer can negotiate like a bulldog. Usually a seller cannot. Again, this is because a buyer can usually walk if they are unhappy, whereas a seller must find another buyer if there is no sale.

However, a seller does have the issue of time to his advantage. Everyone has a limited amount of time. Nothing could be more obvious. Well, for a buyer, this has a cost, because if a buyer cannot make a deal work, she must go on to the next seller, and try again. And if that seller cannot make a deal or does not have what she needs, he must move on again...and again.

For most buyers, this a nightmare. Unless they are simply having fun with the buying process (and some people actually do), there is a strong likelihood the buyer simply wants to find the right product or service at the right price and get it done. Negotiating can be tiring and take away from other productive uses of one's time.

A clever seller keeps this truth in mind at all times. He will engage with the buyer in every way possible, giving him total focus and attention and immersing him in the process of buying as much as he possibly can, for as long as he can, so that he will not be inclined to end the process and go somewhere else and start the whole thing over.

As a seller, you remind the buyer how much he has learned about your product or service, how much you have devoted yourself to working through the deal, and how much more you are willing to do to see a beneficial result for both parties.

Now some sellers push this concept by claiming deadlines, such as a sale ending in 10 hours, or competition, such as another buyer who is waiting to make an offer on the same product, but often these are disingenuous methods of pushing buyers to buy before considering further.

These methods may work, but if they are false, but if a buyer learns of this method, you may lose a customer for life. It is better to be straightforward and tell the buyer about something imminent if it is true, but never use it to push buyer to a decision.

Just as a buyer can make productive use of negotiating skills, a seller can employ methods to give him a greater likelihood of success. Negotiating is a crucial element of buying and selling almost anything, and those who know the principles are most often the ones who realize the profitable deals.

Negotiation Skills Training

Negotiating is "The process by which two or more parties with different needs and goals work to find a mutually acceptable solution to an issue"

In order for us to get what we're looking for, this is a skill that we can't pass up. It does not matter if you have the best business skills out there. You'll always benefit from learning effective negotiating skills in order to advance your success.

5 Effective Negotiating Technique

Here are five techniques. These techniques aim to ensure a positive negotiation process.

1. **Be Confident** - Disregard how badly you want an outcome from your negotiations. If the other party thinks you are desperate, they will be in a stronger position which gives you less leverage over the situation.

2. **Arrive Prepared** - Before entering a negotiation, consider all the variables that may come up. Expect issues to come up and when they do end the negotiations and learn more about the new matter before starting the negotiation again.

3. **Build a Buffer** - Never begin a negotiation with what you're ultimately trying to achieve. Give yourself an ample "cushion" between what you're requesting and what it is that you actually want. This allows you to compromise and not give up anything important which also shows the other party that you are flexible.

4. **Understand Your Limits** - Before the negotiations begin figure out what your absolute minimum offer is and don't be afraid to leave the negotiations if you can't get your minimum.

5. **Remain Composed** - If negotiations start to get heated, simply walk away and take a few minutes to gather your thoughts and re-assess your situation. If the other party refuses to agree on a compromise then consider what is more beneficial: continue or simply end the negotiations.

Chapter IV

Negotiating Skills Enhancement

Negotiation skills are not only important in the business sector, they are also important in our social lives perhaps for deciding a time to meet, or where to go on a rainy day, etc. It is usually considered as a compromise to settle an argument or an issue to benefit ourselves as much as possible.

Be as creative as possible

Brainstorming, listening to outlandish proposals and opening up to unanticipated possibilities make negotiation skills more effective. If we were to respond with new ideas and do the unexpected, this would open doors to far greater gains than when we behave predictably. Creativity can make just about everyone look good.

Be conscious

Consciousness of the difference between positions and interests is among the most important negotiation skills. Great negotiators are people who can figure out why they want something - and why the other party wants their outcome - that is what looking at interest is. These interests are what lasting agreements are made of.

Always be fair

If the party you are negotiating with feel a process is fair, they're more likely to make real commitments. They are also less likely to walk away from the negotiations or agreement reached. To make sure there is fairness, sometimes the two teams are helped when a neutral, external authority or mediator.

Listen actively

One of the bad negotiation skills is spending all of your listening time planning how to get back out at the other party. This means when they finally stop talking, you have not heard them. It is a good negotiation skill to focus on what others say, both on their words and their underlying meaning because this will help you understand the interests upon which agreement can be based.

BATNA

BATNA stands for the Best Alternative to a Negotiated Agreement and it simply means that if you can improve things on your own, you don't need to negotiate. However, BATNA is not your bottom line and is only a measure of the relative value of negotiating a particular issue with a particular party, or whether you can fall back on a better alternative.

Commitment

Never make a commitment unless you can fulfill it. This is one of the most undervalued negotiation skills although it is important. You should note that commitment is not likely if one party feels that the process has not been fair.

Chapter V

10 Reasons to Improve Your Negotiation Skills

There's a certain amount of trepidation in entering the marketplace with a new product or service, or expanding into new markets, which is why good negotiation skills are vital. There are many unknown factors in dealing with new and unfamiliar business territory, and how you are able to handle negotiating them can spell the difference between success and failure.

An investment in rigorous negotiation training can pay off handsomely when it comes to developing your negotiation skills.

Actually, business - like international diplomacy - is really based on negotiating. It is no coincidence that the Spanish word for "business" in virtually every Latin American country is negocios.

Business negotiation skills that have not been properly developed and honed to a fine edge can fall prey to intimidation and often result in surrendering on issues that you may not have wanted or needed.

In fact, business negotiations are all about give and take, ultimately resulting in a solution that is satisfactory to everyone. Negotiation training is the most effective way to "level the playing field."

Here are 10 reasons to improve your negotiation skills

1. Choosing a negotiation strategy instead of an adversarial approach preserves relationships and builds trust.

2. It is better to negotiate solutions than to leave matters in the hands of panels of arbitrators who don't have first-hand knowledge of the student.

3. Negotiation ensures that both sides find common ground. As part of the process, you will be surprised to find out how many things you already agree on.

4. Negotiating solutions saves money because there is no need to hire expensive lawyers.

5. The negotiation process allows each side to hear and address the other side's fears and concerns. Once that is done solutions will emerge.

6. Negotiation allows each side to think about an alternative solution that might be agreeable to the other side.

7. Negotiation is always more successful than confrontation. The solutions may not be exactly the ones that you had in mind before the process started, but since both sides agree on them, they are more likely to be successfully implemented.

8. Negotiation ensures that both sides communicate and focus on the important issues.

9. The negotiation process is quicker at finding solutions than hearings and appeals.

10. Successful negotiation leads to successful advocacy; meaning that the student's needs are met and parents/guardians maintain a good working relationship with the school.

Chapter VI

Negotiation Skills Training

Quiet honestly, the best way to get negotiating experience is to negotiate in the real world. There are countless opportunities everywhere you go.

It is not advisable to try a new negotiation tactic on a major business deal for the first time, but simply start applying this negotiation tactic in situations where the outcome is not that important.

You could just go into an electronics store and negotiate about the price of a plasma TV, or a car dealership and bargain about the price. These are the best training environments, because you'll get real-life experience from people who are professional negotiators.

Negotiation Skill Training In Hypnosis

Imagine you are sitting across the table from someone you are negotiating with. This could be a negotiation for the purchase of a business, the sale of a car, or just trying to get your kids to do their chores.

In any negotiation, you want the other party to do what you want and by the same token, they want you to do what they want. So how do you tilt the scales in your favor?

Well quite simply, you have to become a better negotiator. Contrary to what people may think, this is a skill that can be taught. You just have to be willing to learn.

If you are ready to learn and want to invest the time, effort and money necessary to become a better negotiator, then keep reading. Otherwise, stop reading right now! Negotiation skill training is not for you.

I don't mean to be harsh, but that is the reality of it. If you want to continue losing negotiations in your everyday life, then don't work on it.

But if you are still reading, then this information is for you.

Just like master mechanics have an arsenal of tools in their toolboxes, master negotiators must also have different weapons that they call on to win negotiations.

One weapon that you can have at your disposal is the power of hypnosis. Say what?

That's right, I said hypnosis. Now I know what you are thinking.

You will have to waive a gold watch in front of the car salesman and count to ten, at which point he will get very sleepy. Then he will lose all ability to think for himself and you can get your new car for half off.

No, that's great for the movies, but that's not how it works. Let me explain it this way...put yourself in the other person's shoes for a minute.

In order for that person to give you what you want, what is the first thing that will have to happen? They have to like you.

Think about it.

From the other person's perspective, if they look at you and see a mean, grouchy person, will that give them any reason to give you what you want? Of course not.

However, if you form a good rapport with them and they see you as a friend, wouldn't they be more flexible in a negotiation? Usually yes and at the very least, it can't hurt.

As you probably know, this is the Rapport Step in sales and negotiation. This is where you get to know the other person as a person and not just someone you are about to negotiate with.

If you already know this person well, like a family member, then the rapport step is necessary to dig deeper and get more information about the topic you are negotiating about. This is so that you can understand where that person is coming from and use that to your advantage.

What does this have to do with hypnosis?

My point is that what the marketers are calling hypnosis is not hypnosis in the way that we traditionally think of it. It is just a series of steps (like the rapport step) and mental cues that you can use the persuade the other party to give you what you want in a negotiation.

Don't get me wrong, even though you may not be able to get someone to dance like a chicken in front of 300 people, these techniques are still very powerful and can give you the edge in a negotiation.

Chapter VII

Negotiating Skills and Career Development

Negotiating skills in career development are almost like the lifeline of your career. You need to master the art of negotiating if you want to get ahead in your career and in everything that you do. Communication forms a very crucial part when it comes to developing the skills.

Negotiating has a very clear and simple definition which is to reach an understanding with another person where both of you are fully satisfied. In many professions today, people are losing out just because they have not truly polished their skills.

Areas of Application

Negotiating skills come to play in many areas of our lives. However, when it comes to career and business, the skills will mean winning or losing a deal. In your work place or business, you negotiate how work is shared, various prices of commodities, how to undertake work and the list is endless.

However, it is also vital to apply the skills well in our personal lives. For example, you may negotiate where to invest with your spouse or where to go for lunch. All these little things form the basis of strong skills. Charity begins at home and if you have good skills at home, you will translate that in your career.

How to negotiate well

Negotiating skills are governed by different rules. To maximize these skills in your career, you need to know how to negotiate with clients and colleagues. The first rule is to understand the other party. A good negotiator will understand their need and know how to meet it.

To negotiate effectively with the other party, your needs must be well known. Do not assume that they know your needs. Do this in the most thoughtful way and you will discover the full power of good negotiation.

Once you have spelt out your needs and you have considered the needs of the other party, it is time to come to an understanding. During many instances of your career, you will discover that there are no straight-forward solutions; you have to negotiate your way to a deal and so on.

This is a stage that will require plenty of flexibility from either party. You need to reach an understanding that will serve you both fairly. Good thinking skills and communication ability will come to play. Finally, you will reach an agreement that is satisfying to both parties.

Chapter VIII

The Importance of Good Negotiation Skills to Your Business Success

Having good negotiation skills can be the difference between success and failure in the business world. Those that know how to negotiate tend to rise to the top of whatever industry they are in. At the same time, those that do not know how to negotiate tend to stay where they are or fall backwards.

If you want to be successful in the industry, a study of developing negotiation skills should be at the forefront of your mind. Here are a few things to consider about the importance of good negotiation skills to your business success.

One of the primary benefits of having good negotiation skills is that you will be able to save money. If you represent your business or if you are negotiating for yourself, you will be able to negotiate a cheaper price when buying something.

When making large purchases, you need to be able to negotiate with the sales representative and get a better price. If you simply take the price that is being offered to you, it is very possible that will be taken advantage of. Learning how to negotiate will allow you to save substantial amounts of money over a period of time.

Another important reason for developing good negotiation skills is that you will be able to make more money for your business as well. If you are trying to sell a product or secure a contract, you need to be able to negotiate in order to make it happen. By doing this, you will be able to secure a larger selling price and increase your profit margins. Increasing profit margins is one of the biggest objectives for most businesses. If you can learn how to do this, you will be invaluable to your employer and this will be directly related to your business success.

In addition to being a better negotiator, you will also develop several other traits that are essential in business. Many of the same skills that you use in negotiation will translate over to other areas of the business.

For example, when learning good negotiation skills, you will learn how to be an effective listener. In order to be successful in negotiation, you have to be able to listen to the other person to see what they want.

This skill will be very valuable to you in other areas of the business. If you are a manager, you will need to be able to listen to your employees to see what motivates them.

If you are dealing with customers, you need to be able to listen to what they are telling you so that you can find a product or service that matches their needs.

When you are aiming to achieve business success, developing good negotiation skills should be at the top of your priority list. This is by far one of the most important skills that you can develop as a businessperson. It can easily take you from where you currently are to where you eventually want to be.

Chapter IX

Leadership Development Through Negotiation Skills

Negotiation is the foundation of relationship at professional and personal front. Most importantly, if you are negotiating at professional levels, a diplomatic approach is must, you just cannot unveil your thoughts as you do in friendly conversations in everyday life.

Often you have to resort to symbolism rather than using the direct method of speaking your heart out verbally. It is not solely your skillfulness that determines your leadership quality, but your negotiation skills actually determine how proficient you are in handling your tasks.

Leadership Development through skilful Negotiation

There are many negotiation development training courses that actually teach you how to maneuver and tackle your negotiation traits with various parties. It is quite a critical task to master negotiation skills but you can achieve success in doing so through leadership development training classes.

While negotiating, there are a few important factors that you should consider. First, take into consideration the person or persons with whom you are going to negotiate. A leadership development class will help you acknowledge the person with whom you are negotiating.

Once you determine the right person, you need to envision the number of days you have to continue relationship. The tenure will determine the process and quality of negotiation.

Your negotiation development classes will then help you take note of the different issues and options that are associated with the parties. Then, dissect each issue and envision the length of discussion that each issue demands.

Remember, these are the complex situations and these can only be handled with leadership development training courses.

Once you attend the negotiation development class, you will realize that different negotiations demand different settings. Sometimes some form of negotiation requires a third party to carry forward the negotiation task on behalf of other parties.

For instance, there is a negotiation that needs to be accomplished between two parties. In that case, a third party is required to bore the negotiation between the two parties.

A manager or a supervisor can only solve problems through negotiation skills. Leadership development skills bring cooperation between the networks of people. Hence, once you complete leadership development training course, you realize the importance of communication and how it helps in enhancing leadership skills.

Remember, negotiation can be an accomplished management tool to ensure that all management task is fulfilled with dexterity. A leadership development training course implicates that, to acquire leadership talent, you need to negotiate properly, but along with it you also need to understand the various intricacies of negotiation.

Research shows, that negotiation is an accomplished management tool and therefore the first thing taught in any leadership development class is how to negotiate.

Nevertheless, you will want to attend a negotiation development training class to ensure a prospective career for yourself. Hence, negotiation is the skill that requires continuous attention at every step of organizational development.

Negotiating Skills for Real Estate Professionals

Negotiating skills are crucial to dealing with everyday situations, both at work and at home. When I first became active in creative real estate, I realized my negotiating skill set was very weak and needed immediate improvement.

As any seasoned, real estate professional will tell you, honing your negotiation skills is like giving yourself an immediate raise. And learning to listen effectively is one of the most important skills you can master.

Clearly the skills involved in negotiation and effective listening are close cousins. Both are vital for a successful career. Henry Kissinger, one of the United States most respected negotiators, commented that listening is the key to success at the bargaining table.

In negotiations, we often concentrate on positions rather than interests. The result is an outcome that does not extract the greatest possible value out of the process. Moreover, you may inadvertently damage an important relationship. Effective negotiation dramatically affects the perceived value of the goods or services we are buying or selling. When you're selling, it raises the perceived value of your product or service. When buying, it can lower the perceived value. Whether buying or selling, the style of negotiation is of prime importance.

Every negotiation involves an element of conflict: Two sides must face-off before any negotiation can begin. When a high degree of concern is expressed for the substance of the negotiation and a low degree of concern is expressed for the relationship of the parties, a defeatist behavior pattern is produced.

This is characterized by pressure, intimidation, adversarial relationships and an attempt to get as much as possible as soon as possible.

Avoiding defeatist attitudes at the negotiating table is simply a matter of a little planning. Find something in the deal that is not important to you but is important for your counterpart.

When things are getting sticky and about to spiral out of control, concede the unimportant element to your counterpart. Often times, this is enough to clinch the deal in your favor. It will, at least, allow you to proceed in a more constructive manner.

And while your planning, ensure you have an exit strategy. If everything goes against you, you will be saved by this little bit of contingency planning.

Improving your communication skills means not just becoming a better listener, but learning to listen to what is not being said. It is said that 90% of communication is non-verbal. If you've nothing to say, stay silent. Learn to emphasize or reinforce what you are saying through your body language and demeanor. Carefully watch your conterpart's body language to gauge what they are really thinking.

As always, practice makes perfect so set some time aside with your colleagues to work through some negotiating games and training. Your negotiating skills will improve quickly if you practice when you're not under the gun.

Last but not least, the better your negotiating skill set, the easier and more enjoyable your relationships will be. You will find that it's easier to agree and, more importantly, to disagree with each other.

Ultimately, you'll be far better prepared to negotiate the curves that life throws your way.

Negotiation Skills and Influencing Other's Perceptions

A very key element in negotiation involves learning what is key to negotiation. It's not redundancy. Its truth.

The process to learn effective negotiation skills is like an attempt to climb a sheer rock wall. It can be done, it has been done, but the sooner one identifies solid places to put her foot or grab a ledge, the faster... and more safely... the wall is scaled.

Similarly, the sooner the "key" concepts are learned, the faster and safer the path to successful negotiation.

One foundational "key" issue in successful negotiation is perceptions. Learn the way these mold the process and you will learn how to use them to your advantage, every time.

Perceptions are present in a negotiation whether people want them to be there or not. The fact is, whether a negotiation is happening over the telephone between two different parties on two different continents or whether it is happening in a crowded, dimly lit lounge on leather couches, there will be perceptions of each party by the other party and those perceptions will influence the process and the outcome, in a big way.

In a previous article, I talked about the attitudes and actions of negotiators that can help or hinder the reaching of a successful agreement. But there is more to negotiation skills than just the perception of the other party's attitude. They include the perception of their perceptions.

What does the other party perceive you will do? What are they going to do if you surprise them? What are they going to do if you play it exactly as they would have planned? These are questions that will arise in the mind of the parties. The real issue here is whether you can influence the other party's perceptions before they act on them.

The fact is, you can. You can do it honestly and legitimately and if you are good, the other party will have no idea it was planned.

There may be a limitless number of "perceptions" the other party will have of you, and here we will address a few. Learning about how to influence one perception will show you how to actively influence almost any that could surface in a typical negotiation scenario.

Accepting the first opening offer - consider what will happen in a negotiation when the buyer makes an offer, and the seller immediately takes it. What is the feeling (perception) created in the buyer? Does he think he just made a good deal, or does he become worried he just offered too much? In truth, the buyer will often react with fear when his offer is immediately accepted. He wonders if he was too aggressive. Too positive. Too hopeful. He wonders if maybe he really did not know the true value of the item for sale and that is why the seller had no hesitation to accept.

Learning successful negotiation skills will show you that accepting the opening offer is often a bad idea. This is because people expect to negotiate, even if it's only a little.

So if the seller accepts without complaint or condition, it creates fear and anxiety in the buyer's mind that there is something she doesn't know about, something that should have been researched.

Otherwise, why no debate over the price? Once a buyer feels this way, the gloves come off. Then the parties are in a fight mode because the buyer has this gnawing feeling that she was just taken... and doesn't even know why.

Become an astute seller by not accepting the opening offer, even if you want to. This is the time to get creative. It may be that you are going to come back requesting a small concession of the buyer, something like a shorter escrow or a larger deposit or a higher interest rate.

Whatever it is, significant or insignificant, ask for a concession, even if you like the present agreement as it stands.

This methodology influences the other party's perceptions (in this case, the buyer). It tells them (without telling them) you are still moving toward a deal, and that they don't need to worry that they just fell for a trap you set.

Remember: negotiation is a process.

Making concessions - consider how the opposing party would feel if you made absolutely no concessions to your terms of the deal. How will that influence their perception of you? Will it make the other party defensive?

Concessions are necessary; the other side expects them. If you don't make them, they will sense you are not going to budge on anything. And that is not what you want them thinking, even if it's true.

Every known seller will present something for sale, and after he receives an offer, he raised his price? The average reaction of buyers in this situation is something between bewilderment and anger, and rightfully so. To take this position is simply insulting to the other party.

Well, making zero concessions isn't much better. To work out a successful deal, you have to have concessions built into your negotiation. In other words, you have to have concessions planned, concessions that you will make as the process goes along.

Don't overlook this point. It is very important. The main reason to have concessions planned is simply this: you don't get any credit for concessions you don't bring up.

If you make your offer and load everything you would possibly give in to in that offer... you have nothing to work with down the road in the negotiation.

You can't deplete your ammo at the first sight of the enemy or you'll have nothing to shoot with later on. And the carelessness could get you killed.

So how to do this? Make a systematic plan on paper or in your mind of what you will give, what you can concede. Put in order of priority.

Then, as the negotiation proceeds, pull out the smaller, less important concessions first. The other side will push again, asking for more.

Proceed to the heavier ones, the ones that cost you more. But each time you give up something, you will make certain you are getting what is important to you in the deal, and you are getting closer and closer to a successful completion.

Putting the plan into action is what it's all about. And there's no way to put a plan into action if there isn't a plan. So do yourself a huge favor and before you get into any negotiation, large or small, make a plan of how you will influence the other party's perception of you and how you are going to negotiate. Try it; you'll perceive the difference right away.

Negotiating Skills and the 10 Powers of Negotiation: The Critical Role of Lateral Thinking

Does anyone doubt that men and woman are sometimes different, or that they sometimes view the world differently? Has anyone experienced how men and women can sometimes have different perceptions of the same event?

Can anyone seriously dispute that men and women sometimes approach relationships quite differently? So, why is this? And why is this even remotely relevant in the context of negotiation?

After spending more than 30 years negotiating agreements around the world and after researching Nelson Mandela's approach to his historic negotiations with the South African apartheid government, I identified 10 Powers of Negotiation. These 10 Powers reveal the critical role of lateral thinking in the negotiating process by highlighting that negotiators need both left and right-brain skills.

You will notice that some require predominantly left-brain skills and others require predominantly right-brain skills. But, to pull all the Powers together, negotiators require a combination of both.

These are the 10 Powers:

- The power of understanding that a negotiation is a process.
- The power of preparation.
- The power of positioning.
- The power of common sense and logic.
- The power of dignity, congeniality, humility and humor.
- The power of truth and fairness.
- The power of observation - of listening and seeing.
- The power of morality, courage and attitude.
- The power of patience.
- The power to walk away.

The advantages of lateral thinking

Because lateral thinkers are people who have the ability to use both the left and right sides of their brain, they have significantly more insight into human behavior than those who are not lateral thinkers.

They not only see unusual patterns of behavior that others might miss, they also have a more nuanced and layered sense of what is happening around them. Because of this, they also see more options for problem solving and have far superior problem solving skills than those who are not lateral thinkers.

And because the negotiating process is about identifying the problems each side is hoping to solve, the identification of the problems and finding different options and approaches to solving those problems lie at the very core of any successful negotiation.

Lateral thinking and empathy

Nelson Mandela's negotiating skills and experiences highlight the enormous importance of looking at every negotiation through the eyes of those with whom you are negotiating. He saw the enormous advantages that this can present on many different levels in a negotiation.

His life is a remarkable window into his lateral thinking skills. It is quite fascinating how he honed these skills during his life and how he used them in his negotiations with the South African government.

When it comes to being able to see the world through the other side's eyes, empathy is the name of the game. While it might be tempting to argue, using left-brain skills, that a position the other side is taking is "logical" or "illogical" or "black-and-white," almost invariably the right-brain skills are far more telling and useful.

Clearly, to get into someone's head we need to tap into their emotional state and understand it. We need to tap into whatever intuitive skills we can muster.

This is why we either have to develop both left-brain and right-brain skills, or we have to assemble negotiating teams that possess these skills.

How lateral thinking exposes the risk of negotiating alone

I've accepted that I'm a predominantly left-brain person. I think of myself as logical and rational - perhaps to a fault. I've also always accepted the problem that this almost inevitably creates, and the opportunities that I might lose as a result.

I've therefore accepted the absolute need to work on my right-brain functionality. Unfortunately, what I've sometimes found is that, as I began to focus on my right-brain development, I often found myself taking my eye off my left-brain functionality. I needed to find a solution to this - and I did.

I decided that, whenever possible, I would never negotiate alone. Instead, I wanted at my side the smartest right-brain negotiator I could find - as well as the smartest left-brain negotiator to keep me focused.

As the 10 Powers of Negotiation highlights, negotiators have to keep their eyes on my different balls simultaneously. And as they have to observe and listen to the other side's negotiating team, and particularly when that team is sometimes quite large, it is almost impossible to do this alone.

To have a team of left and right-brain negotiators watching and listening and assessing what is happening is a huge advantage and will always yield a better result than handling this alone.

Chapter X

Effective Negotiation Skills

1. Be an alert negotiator. A successful negotiator must be assertive and open to challenge everything. Skilled negotiators know that everything can be negotiated. Challenging is not synonymous with refusing all the offers given by an opponent. All offers must be analyzed separately.

You must ask the right questions when an offer is given. This implies that you have to be critical about everything you read in the newspapers and see on television. You will not be able to negotiate if you cannot challenge the validity of the information exposed by your opponent.

Being assertive means that you need to ask the right questions in order to gather all the information you need to know. You are also not willing to always say "NO" for an answer. Train yourself to hide your feelings of anxiety or anger. Let others know what you want without feeling threatened. Train yourself to use "I" messages. For example, change "I do not want you to do that" into "I feel uncomfortable when you do that."

Realize that there is a big difference between assertiveness and aggressiveness. You need to become assertive when you defend your own interests while respecting the interests of others at the same time. If you do not show consideration in the interests of others, you will look aggressive. Assertiveness is part of effective negotiations.

2. Be a good listener. A good negotiator is like a detective. They often ask probing questions and then listen. The other negotiator will inform you about everything you need to know; the only you have to do is listen.

Many conflicts can be solved easily if we try to learn to the words of others. We are too often busy speaking and forget to listen to the words of others. You can become an effective listener by letting others speak. Follow the 70/30 rule: 70 percent of the time is used for listening and 30 percent for speaking. Stimulate the other negotiator to speak with open questions: these questions cannot be answered by simple "yes" or "no."

3. Be prepared. Acquire as much information related to the negotiation at hand. What are their needs? What pressures are they experiencing? What kind of options do they have? Knowledge about all these will strengthen your position when facing the "opponent." In short, the more information you have, the more prepared you will be for the "war."

4. Set a high target. Good negotiators will set a high target to get the best out their negotiations. If you expect to get a lot, you will end up with a lot. A good negotiator is always optimistic. All sales persons usually ask for more than what they expect and all buyers will offer less than what they are willing to pay for.

5. Always be patient. If we want to persuade someone, we must be flexible with the time we have. Our patience will be advantageous if the other negotiator is in a hurry. Always thin rationally. Do not be reckless in making important decisions. This will have a big impact on your future.

6. Focus on satisfaction. Help the other negotiator to become satisfied. Satisfaction means that their primary interests are fulfilled. Do not confuse the primary interests with their desires. Try to accommodate their needs.

7. Do not make the first move. The best way to find out the aspirations the other negotiators is to persuade them to make the first move. You might be asking less than you thought. If you start with an initial offer, you might be offering them more than they need.

8. Do not accept the first offer. If you accept the first offer, the other negotiators will think that they have won. They will be more satisfied when you refuse to accept their first offer. If you say "yes" to their first offer, they will think that they have successfully pushed you to the limits of your abilities.

9. Do not make easy concessions. If you make concessions, try to get the other negotiator to also make concessions in exchange. "I shall do this if you do that." This tactic will usually make your opponents uncomfortable. They will think that you are smart and have a strong position.

10. Do not hesitate to back off. Do not negotiate without options. Prepare yourself for the worst outcome. Prepare several options as alternative strategies you have during the negotiations. This will give you the chance to think and reconsider the offers of your opponents. If you lose, you can at least say to yourself that you have done your best in the negotiation process.

Conclusion

In most negotiations, you will find the parties involved are not on the same footing when compared with each other; they have a difference in status. Understanding this element of negotiation is an important part of learning successful negotiation skills.

So what is status and what does it mean to a negotiation? In short, status means position. It defines where one party stands in relation to the other party. And really, it has nothing to do with economic or social standing at all. The status of a negotiator is solely determined only by his position in relation to the negotiator on the other side.